DATE DUE	

Pocahontas

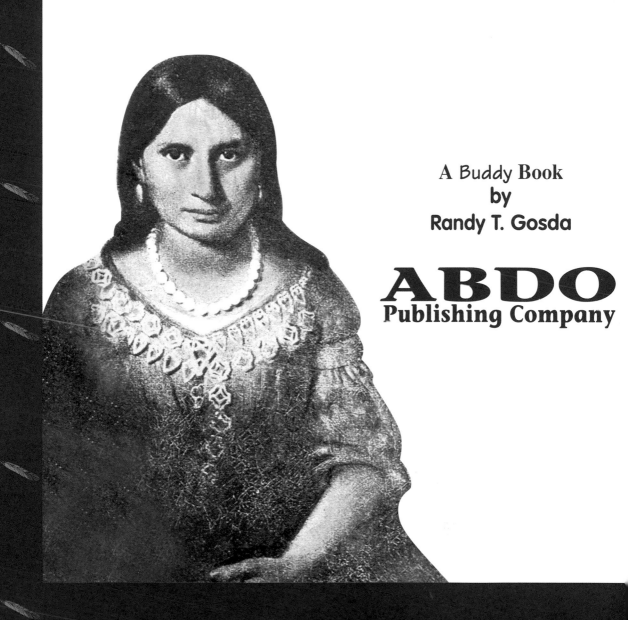

A Buddy Book
by
Randy T. Gosda

ABDO
Publishing Company

VISIT US AT

www.abdopub.com

Published by Buddy Books, an imprint of ABDO Publishing Company, 4940 Viking Drive, Suite 622, Edina, Minnesota 55435. Copyright © 2002 by Abdo Consulting Group, Inc. International copyrights reserved in all countries. No part of this book may be reproduced in any form without written permission from the publisher.

Printed in the United States.

Edited by: Christy DeVillier
Contributing Editors: Matt Ray, Michael P. Goecke
Image Research: Deborah Coldiron, Susan Will
Graphic Design: Jane Halbert
Cover Photograph: North Wind Picture Archives
Interior Photographs/Illustrations: North Wind Picture Archives, Denise Esner

Library of Congress Cataloging-in-Publication Data

Gosda, Randy T., 1959-
    Pocahontas / Randy T. Gosda.
      p. cm. — (First biographies. Set II)
    Includes index.
    Summary: A brief biography of the seventeenth-century Indian princess who befriended Captain John Smith and the English settlers of Jamestown.
    ISBN 1-57765-732-2
    1. Pocahontas, d.1617—Juvenile literature. 2. Powhatan Indians—Biography—Juvenile literature. [1. Pocahontas, d. 1617. 2. Powhatan Indians—Biography. 3. Indians of North America—Virginia—Biography. 4. Women—Biography. 5. Smith, John, 1580-1631. 6. Jamestown (Va.)—History.] I. Title.

E99.P85 P57347 2002
975.5'01'092—dc21
[B]

                           2001034932

Table Of Contents

Who Is Pocahontas?

Pocahontas is a famous peacemaker. She helped early American settlers get along with American Indians. Another word for American Indian is Native American.

America remembers Pocahontas the peacemaker.

Pocahontas lived in America before it was a country. That was more than 400 years ago.

Pocahontas was born around 1595. Her real name was Matoaka. Pocahontas was her nickname. Pocahontas means playful little girl.

Pocahontas was an American Indian.

The Powhatan Indians

Pocahontas's father was Chief Powhatan. Chief Powhatan ruled about 28 Indian tribes. The Powhatan tribes lived near the Chesapeake Bay. The Chesapeake Bay is in Virginia.

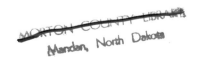

Pocahontas's people hunted, fished, and farmed. They hunted deer with bows and arrows. They caught fish with spears, nets, and traps. The Powhatans grew corn, beans, and squash.

The Powhatans fished with spears and nets.

Jamestown

In 1607, people from England sailed to America. These English people built a settlement on the James River. This settlement was Jamestown. Jamestown is one of the first American settlements. Jamestown was close to many Powhatan villages.

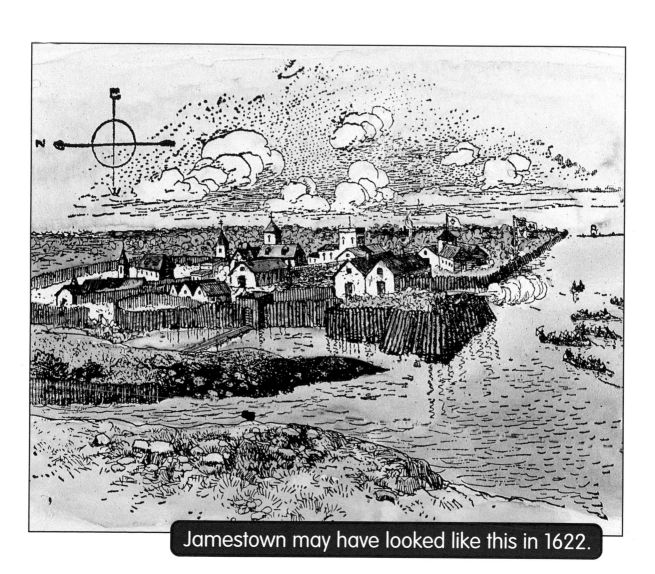

Jamestown may have looked like this in 1622.

Life was hard for the Jamestown settlers. They did not have much food. So, the settlers traded with the Powhatan Indians. These American Indians gave the settlers corn. The settlers gave the Indians metal tools. But the settlers did not trust the Powhatans. They called the Powhatan Indians savages.

The Powhatans traded food for tools.

Saving John Smith

   Captain John Smith was one of Jamestown's rulers. One day, John Smith left Jamestown to look for food. A Powhatan Indian caught John Smith. This Powhatan Indian was Pocahontas's brother. His name was Opechancanough. Opechancanough brought John Smith to Chief Powhatan.

Captain John Smith

John Smith said that Chief Powhatan almost killed him. A young girl begged Chief Powhatan not to hurt John Smith. This young girl was Pocahontas. Young Pocahontas may have saved John Smith's life. This is the famous Pocahontas legend. No one is sure this legend is true.

Did Pocahontas save John Smith's life?

A Kidnapping

Pocahontas often visited Jamestown. She played with the Jamestown children. Pocahontas brought food to the settlers. Pocahontas liked the Jamestown settlers. But not all Powhatans got along with the settlers.

The settlers and the Indians battled each other.

The settlers were living on Chief Powhatan's land. So, Chief Powhatan wanted to rule the settlers. But the settlers wanted the Powhatans to follow England's rules. So, the settlers and the Powhatans began fighting. Chief Powhatan kept some settlers as prisoners.

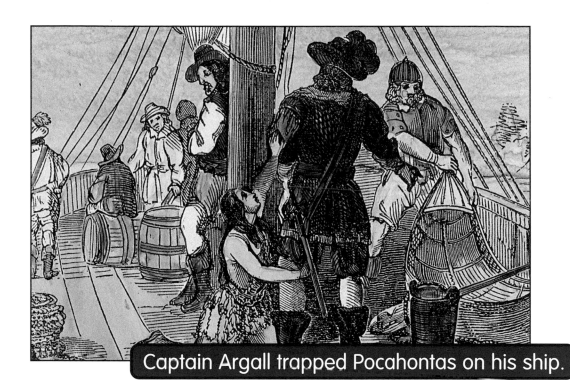

Captain Argall trapped Pocahontas on his ship.

In 1613, Captain Argall kidnapped Pocahontas. He took Pocahontas to Jamestown. The settlers hoped to trade Pocahontas. Would Chief Powhatan trade the English prisoners for his favorite daughter? Chief Powhatan said no.

Changing Into Rebecca

Pocahontas was angry with the settlers. She wanted to go home. But the settlers kept her in Jamestown. They turned Pocahontas into an English lady. The settlers taught Pocahontas English manners. The settlers dressed Pocahontas in English clothes. The settlers taught Pocahontas to be a Christian. Pocahontas's new Christian name was Rebecca.

Pocahontas may be the first American Indian Christian.

Peace Of Pocahontas

John Rolfe was a tobacco farmer in Jamestown. John and Pocahontas became friends. John Rolfe wanted to marry Pocahontas. He told Chief Powhatan. The chief allowed John to marry Pocahontas. Then, Chief Powhatan offered to make peace with the settlers. Peace lasted for eight years. We call this time the Peace of Pocahontas.

Pocahontas and Thomas

Pocahontas married John Rolfe on April 5, 1614. Pocahontas had a son one year later. His name was Thomas.

A Trip To England

In 1616, Pocahontas sailed to England. Pocahontas met the king and queen. She saw London Bridge and Westminster Abbey. Pocahontas saw many things she had never seen before.

Pocahontas met King James I.

The English liked Pocahontas. So, the English gave money to Jamestown. Many of them wanted to move to Jamestown. Jamestown grew very big, thanks to Pocahontas.

Pocahontas never saw Jamestown again. She became too sick to sail home. Pocahontas died around the age of 22.

Pocahontas the peacemaker did a lot in her short life. America will not forget how she helped the Jamestown settlers. This is why the legend of Pocahontas lives today.

Pocahontas the peacemaker

Important Dates

1595 Pocahontas is born around this time.

April 26, 1607 People from England arrive on the shore of North America.

June 15, 1607 Chief Powhatan meets the Jamestown settlers for the first time.

1613 The Jamestown settlers carry off Pocahontas.

April 5, 1614 Pocahontas marries John Rolfe.

1615 Pocahontas and John Rolfe have a son. They name him Thomas Rolfe.

Spring 1616 Pocahontas, John Rolfe, Thomas, and many Powhatans sail to England.

March 21, 1617 Pocahontas dies. Her grave is in Gravesend, England.

Important Words

American Indian Native Americans, the very first people to live in America.

Christian someone who believes in Jesus Christ.

kidnap to carry off someone against their will.

legend an old story that many believe, but cannot be proven true.

prisoner someone who is locked up.

savages people who have a wild way of life.

Web Sites

History of Jamestown
www.apva.org/history/index.html
Learn more about Pocahontas, John Rolfe, John Smith, Chief Powhatan, and the Jamestown settlers at this site.

Jamestown Colony Timeline
www.look.net/gunstonelem/GunstonElemF/Jamestown.html
See Jamestown come to life in this timeline, illustrated by fourth-graders, of Jamestown events from 1607 to 1620.

Index